RADIO POEMS

Sketch of Robin Bell

Radio Poems

ROBIN BELL

PETERLOO POETS

First published in 1989
by Peterloo Poets
2 Kelly Gardens, Calstock, Cornwall PL18 9SA

ISBN 0 905291 98 0

Printed in Great Britain by
Latimer Trend & Company Ltd, Plymouth

ACKNOWLEDGEMENTS

Both *Melville Bay* and *The Other Thief*
have been broadcast on BBC Radio 4.
(Producer John Arnott).

The publisher acknowledges subsidy from the Scottish
Arts Council towards the publication of this volume.

Supported by

Cornwall
County Council

Peterloo Poets is a list published with the assistance of
South West Arts

Contents

CHASING THE BEAR

Despite apparent progress in the nuclear arms talks, Soviet airforce activity in the North Atlantic has increased dramatically.

RAF reports confirm that Tupolev bombers based near Murmansk are now flying up to seven surveillance missions per day along the northern seaboards of Britain and North America. The Russians have recently begun to use a new type of bomber capable of carrying a standoff nuclear weapon.

Their movements are being monitored by the NATO centre at Buchan in the north of Scotland and the Phantom jet fighter force at RAF Leuchars was doubled in 1987 to counter the new Soviet activity. These Phantom jets carry a full war load, including heat-seeking Sidewinder missiles. The Phantom pilots call their sorties 'Chasing the Bear'.

SOC Buchan. 0500 hours 15 March.

(Sound of a lift descending. Its doors open).
Scottish woman officer speaks:

Let the doors shut. What do you hear? Nothing.
Nothing of the storm outside. No ringing phones
or keyboards. The air conditioner. That's a sound.
See that long curved desk? The duty man, hunched down
like a finger on a trigger . . . Radar zones
from Scotland to Russia . . . Map lights winking.

The binders up there on the metal rack:
NATO manuals, Standard Procedures, codes.
All the rituals, like books on how to dance.
Look at the weathercharts. See that front advance?
Typical March. More trees down on the Huntly road.
We're fifty feet underground, safe from attack

from bombs and chemicals, never mind spring gales
—the North Atlantic safe-deposit box.
It's five in the morning. Update the board:
serviceability of Saxa Vord,
Faroes, Benbecula. Plug in those jacks.
Switch on the screen and see if there's some mail.

Ministry of Defence calls this the brain
with radio ears, intelligence, satellite eyes
for quick reaction. Electronic pulse.
Smell that smell? It's seaweed; kelp and dulse
blown against the ventilator grills. Surprised
we don't filter it out? It's good to retain

some sensory input, not digitised
—so the military psychologist says.
The gale's force eight. Good. No reconnaissance
flights by the Russians. They've got more sense.
Bad weather usually makes for quiet days.
It'll be light in Murmansk. Dawn won't rise

here in Buchan for an hour yet.
The Roman legions, stationed on the Wall,
must have felt like this: the northernmost frontier,
wondering when the enemy will appear.
The Soviet monitors can't relax at all,
not since that German pilot, Mathias Rust,

woke them up. Imagine landing in Red Square,
bus drivers gawping, ulcers for the Chiefs of Staff!
. . . The barometer's hit twenty-six. The storm
blew off a shed roof on my fiancé's farm
at tea-time yesterday. He had to move the calves.
Our hours don't match. I'm hardly ever there.

Look at the radar. Something's going on.
. . . Norway's calling . . . There's a Soviet flight
on course for our sector. Not a commercial jet.
We'll send a Phantom up to check it out.
Give Cheltenham co-ordinates for the satellites.
Switch on the Telebrief. "Scramble Q One!"

RAF Leuchars. 0510 hours.

American pilot jumps out of bed:

Mmn. . . Goodbye, dreams. What's the time? Five ten.
Yuk . . . Still pitch dark and blowin' up a storm.
Get dressed. Bunny suit . . . immersion suit.
Get the Mae West on . . . Lace—goddamn these boots!
So where's the Bear? . . Position? . . OK. Confirmed.
Eight minutes to airborne . . . Move it, baby! Run!

11

Into the hangar. There she is, ground crew
already at the wheels to clear the chocks.
... On with the helmet ... Up to the cockpit
... Strap in ... Oxygen ... Radio lines. All set,
Navigator? . . Start engine ... Let's hear those checks.
Anti-icing—yes. Trims—OK. Flaps ... Let's go.

The wind's too high to take off straight ahead.
Hustle her down the taxiway ... Swing round ...
Shee ... Tentsmuir Forest's sawing at the sky ...
Cleared for take-off. Open her up ... Let's fly!
... "Q One to SOC. We're off the ground."
Gon' catch the sucker who's gotten us outta bed.

Bank her round and climb across the coast.
St. Andrews' street lights look pale down below.
Still haven't played golf there. It's almost a year
since I came on attachment ... It's daylight up here,
ice-blue. We've risen above the dawn. There's snow
in those clouds ... Compass ... Course set: north north-east.

Leuchars is history. Wish the kids had stayed.
Marsha called the other wives her tartan cousins.
I took her to that little Norman church.
I said, "You are the keystone of my arch."
—thought she'd like that. She said, "Let's go. I'm frozen."
So how's Newhaven? How was school today?

Has Goodwill gotten your thermal underwear?
No more Burns Suppers to complain about—
"Honey, what *are* these people? Some kinda nuts?
Rutabaga? Sausage in sheep's guts?
That's how Scots recognise romantic poets?"
Keep meanin' to call you. Miss y'all. Take care.

Twenty thousand feet ... Soviet groundbase sees
me flyin' at the Bear. Buchan can tell
every radar blip between here and Murmansk.
So who needs pilots? We all do. Give 'em the chance,
the bureaucrats would do it all themselves.
They'd sit and worry and their brains would freeze;

12

they'd start believing in their own PR
and blow the world to hell through ignorance.
Airmen are safer. When I fly, I see
enemy pilots who look just like me.
They dozy-do around this big square dance
and then relax with their girls at the bar.

I've seen Soviet aircrew so close, when they yawn
you can count their fillings. You get to know a face.
It's like in an elevator: you don't talk;
all you know is the guy lives on your block.
And satellite surveillance! Shee, from out in space
Fort Meade can see a cat and tell if it's a tom!

We're over the oil fields: Beryl . . . Ninian . . . Brent.
It's us—Forty Three Squadron: Fighting Cocks—
who'll protect pipelines if there's a war.
Hey, look! We've radar contact with the Bear.
What type is he? Navigator, betcha five bucks
it's a Bear H . . . Eyeball contact imminent.

Phantom Cockpit. 0600 hours.

English Navigator:

I don't take bets like that. Let's have a look
through the telescope. It's a Bear all right.
Get closer to him till I see what type.
Don't upset him. Let's do it by the book.
Twinkle, twinkle, big red star.
How I wonder what you are?

It's got faired blisters for the cameramen
and a big fat radome. The Bear's airframe
's so ginormous no two are quite the same.
They modify them over and over again.
Can't change a Phantom much. We're packed so neat
I can hardly squeeze my bum into the seat.

13

Noisy bugger! Bears are the only turbo-props
used as strategic bombers. What's he got
for armaments? Let's see you, Rumbleguts.
Dorsal ... ventral ... tail turrets. Cannon up,
locked in the safe position. Let's move close in
... about two hundred feet from his port wing.

He *is* an H Type. Look close. You can tell
where a standoff nuclear kangaroo bomb
can be carried. Just down there. You can cram
twenty thousand pounds conventional bombs as well.
So has he a load on? I'd say niet.
Mind you, I wouldn't like to bet.

So what's he up to? Tracking submarines?
I doubt it. There's the big NATO exercise
coming up. The Soviets will be organised.
More flying hours for us. No sleep between.
Could be the oil rigs he'll inspect,
or just our radar that he wants to check.

He might be going to Cuba for some jaunt.
Jose Marti Airport—named after a poet.
Can you imagine us choosing names like that?
Wordsworth Airport? RAF Betjeman? I can't.
Good luck to you, mates. If I was top banana,
I'd bugger off to a nice warm Havana.

Hold our course tight alongside the Bear.
Time to take snaps for the family album
—GCHQ in Cheltenham.
Begin with the cockpit and work back from there,
Down at sea level, there's still wind and rain.
Up here there's no turbulence. Steady (click). And again.

Your engine noise is awful, Rumbleguts!
I can make out the faces of the crew.
Probably fifteen of them. Just two of us.
See that tail gunner in the big fur hat?
Watch the birdie. There's no mystery.
Click! You've just gone down in history.

Bear Tail Turret. 0615 hours.

Russian Gunner/Photographer.

Our apologies for depriving you
of breakfast, my friends. What would you have chosen?
Porridge, then kippers or bacon and eggs?
Not Leuchars sausages—they're frozen!

We have been told so much about you
—mess menus, recreations, personal profiles.
How do you like your new staff quarters?
Do you know what the carpets cost? It's in our files.

What do we do with all this information?
You may well ask. It just goes round and round
the desks of bureaucrats. They're insatiable,
bumf-addicts, nosey paperhounds.

Maybe I've been doing this job too long.
One more winter in Murmansk will drive me nuts.
You think that Scotland's cold? Huh! We get frostbite
'cause the boilers can't cope in our huts.

If the peace talks work out, I'll get a new posting.
Less nuclear threat, less pilots—that makes sense.
But fewer missiles, more pilots—that makes sense too.
. . . What are you thinking in behind that lens,

do you think we're carrying nuclear weapons?
If we are, do you imagine I'd tell you?
The General Secretary wants to scrap them.
We only have these things because you do.

And you think you have them because of us.
What are you doing? Ah, you're changing reels.
Thirty-six frames of boring sky and metal.
let's see if I've something better to reveal

for your Cheltenham spy centre to analyse.
Look, here's my mug of soup . . . My marking pens.
If you focus very carefully,
you'll see I've got a nice new camera lens.

How about my flying helmet? Quite like yours.
If I put my feet up you can see my boots.
Somewhere in here I've got a letter
headed Biological Research Institute

—it's from my mother. I'll hold it to the window.
From it you will learn many things:
the weather in Smolensk; the colour of grandfather's new gloves
and the date of my cousin's wedding.

Blow up the negative for your translators
—one more file for my family to be in.
They would laugh, particularly grandfather.
He was there when the army stormed Berlin.

He still mimics Winston Churchill.
We were on the same side then.
What will it take—another Hitler?—
till we see some sense again?

Still got a few frames left? Here's a treat.
This'll make your clerks in Cheltenham stare:
Penthouse magazine. Who do you fancy
—the big redhead or the blonde in the deckchair?

Here's value for your taxpayers' money.
Real intelligence! Look at those thighs.
I don't think she's too hairy.
I wonder if you can tell she's got green eyes?

Phantom Cockpit. 0630 hours.

American Pilot:

Shee . . . What's he tryin' to do? Steam up the lens?
Neat trick, a centrefold pinned to the sky.
Get a load of her gazongas! What a chest!
She's got more flotation than my own Mae West!
That gunner who's holdin' her, what's he tryin' to say?
Reflect back our capitalist decadence?

16

Confront us with our female exploitation?
Where'd he get that Penthouse anyways?
He didn't buy it in his corner store.
Russia ain't gotten that liberal, that's for sure.
I'll bet he bought it off some sailor guy
in the Soviet fishing fleet. He's stationed

in Murmansk; so are those Klondike ships
that buy up fish along the Scottish coast.
They land where they like. How 'bout that for security?
In Ullapool pubs, your friendly KGB
drinking with the locals. Like a trading post
—intelligence and blue jeans on every trip.

Cases of scotch, porn, high-tech toy submarines
—Soviet fishermen snap 'em up and ship 'em home.
I guess Russian housewives accept that everything
on the black market stinks of salt herring.
And I'll bet Soviet aircrew distribute them
with kickbacks to the communist machine.

He's gone from the window ... Hey, we're gettin' close
to the oilrigs. Son of a bitch! Was that a trick
to distract us? Oh yeah? You watch my hand ...
You turn your ass around, y'understand,
or I'll cut your nose off. C'mon, take a hike!
Don't you play dumb ... Shit, I can see the Shetland coast.

The Bear is losing height. What's going on?
This is more than just reconnaissance.
He's aiming straight at Sullom Voe
... the oil terminal. He's much too low
—under six thousand feet. It don't make sense.
He knows a Bear can't shake off a Phantom.

I'm ten times as maneuverable, three times as fast.
I can blow him away ... His engine note
is wrong. He's crawling ... still on course
for the oil terminal. I'll have to force
him off before we cross the three mile limit.
What gives, you mother ... Is your pilot juiced?

We've got the situation no-one wants,
when we know exactly what we have to do,
when we've gone right through the usual ritual,
when the rule book says the next step is to kill.
"Come in SOC. Have I clearance from you?
We're well inside the limit ... "

SOC Buchan. 0645 hours

Scottish woman officer:

                          "Hold your fire, Q One!
We haven't authority yet to make a kill.
Stay within missile range and ... Yes I know,
but Cheltenham's issued us an over-ride. They say
their reading of the Bear's telemetry
shows no evidence of hostile ... I know
you can see it with your own eyes. You will

get clearance if and when we hear.
The Bear's having problems with his instruments.
Electrical failure—something of that kind.
The control column ... I know you're not blind.
We mustn't provoke an incident ...
This is *not* an incident. Is that clear?"

The Bear's in trouble. Cheltenham is sure
the main computer's out. Do not attempt
to communicate directly with the Bear.
We must do nothing to make him aware
of how much we can monitor. Right? Nor the extent
his air-to-ground codes are secure.

From now on, use only UHF wave bands.
Please keep your VHF bands clear.
We need to hear the Bear. We mustn't overlook
the possibility he's carrying a nuke.
His signal's weak. His ground control can't hear."
No, we have not got Cheltenham's command ...

18

It's too late anyway to shoot him down.
He's much too close to the oil terminal.
(Please God let him clear the storage tanks!
God save us from trigger-happy Yanks!)
Look at the radar. His speed's down to a crawl.
He's under a thousand feet ... no, he's begun

to climb. Was he faking? Has he kept control
all along? I don't believe that was a game.
"Come in, Cheltenham ... Come in. What's your view?
We have to tell the pilot what to do."
Nothing? Nothing? .. "Q One, you will maintain
the same profile till you clear the terminal."

Bear Tail Turret. 0650 hours.

Russian Gunner/Photographer:

What have you done to us? What invisible weapon
destroys another aircraft from inside?
Our navigator thinks it's a magnetic field
or lasers you've hit us with. The radio has died.

We've no communication with ground control.
Our co-pilot wants to shoot you down
to see if that makes our systems work again.
You make me exchange my cameras for guns.

Cannon to combat-ready. I can see your faces,
your eyes above the oxygen masks. Look, down below,
workers at the oil terminal staring up at us.
They're not taking shelter. They don't know

what's going on. No-one has warned them.
It won't be the first time the generals
sacrifice a few of their own civilians.
But why do it here? To make it plausible

that it's an accident? It would suit
your government to have a good excuse
for cutting down the oil supply. And yet
. . . we're clear of the terminal . I'm confused,

gentlemen, I don't mind admitting it.
Are you attacking us or not? If not,
you must think that we are the aggressors.
So who makes who retaliate?

Where are my dark glasses? I can see you now.
These skinny Sidewinders look like toys.
This will be something to tell your wife about;
a bedtime story for my youngest boy.

I don't believe you'll shoot us down. Not now.
We're over the sea again . . . We're gaining height.
You must know it's the wrong day for us to attack.
When we strike, it will be on a Friday night,

that's when your duty roster's at its thinnest,
when the crews are in the pub. It's bluff
and double bluff. You know we know the weakness;
but it *is* a weakness—that's enough.

We're like an osprey and an Arctic goose
—obvious profiles. Soon both our plumages will change.
We've seen Nellis Base . . . the Mojave Desert Range.
How soon will that Northrop Stealth be introduced?

You and I fly grey, old-fashioned hulks,
like silver bullets for the devil's kin.
But the ferrite on the Stealth's titanium skin
is black as hell—no sound, no light, no bulk.

It will make Star Wars look like arcade games.
We have the specs of Stealth's black flying wing.
Radar and acoustics won't detect a thing—
like trying to see your face in a teflon frying pan.

I've seen the geometry of the Stealth's sub-frame.
I'm impressed—entropy at its most elegant.
You thought you could keep it secret? No, you can't.
We assume you know we're designing one the same.

And we hear your Ministry of Defence won't buy
these new toys for the RAF. They'll let the Americans
foot the whole bill. That's a nice way for an ally
... What's that sound? ... We're losing height again.

The sea's like a ploughed field. The waves are running high.
The water's nearly ... I can feel the cabin yaw ...
The spray is ... I have you in my sights.
If we go down my friends, you're coming too.

Phantom Cockpit. 0705 hours.

English Navigator:

Old Rumbleguts is down ... He's bounced ... He's up again
... A belly-flop ... Oof that'll hurt ... He's ditched.
Look, the tail gunner's ... He's firing! Jesus Christ!
Climb, for God's sake! Climb! ... Get out of range.
Don't shoot back! Just let him drown. Oh fuck,
don't blow him up. He's just a sitting duck.

Don't waste a missile on him. We'd get blamed
for shooting him down. OK? When we get back
We want to show our missiles all intact.
He's rocking on the waves. He can't take aim.
"It's all right, SOC, our hands are clean.
He hasn't touched us either. All serene."

One starboard engine's churning up a spray.
His other props are dead. His cockpit's blurred.
The gunner's stopped. His turret's half-submerged.
Let's see if the crew try to get away.
They've no ejection seats. They could escape
through the hatches ... The Bear's begun to slip

under the water ... almost disappeared.
The tailplane's sticking up into the air
like an iceberg with a big red star.
There's no sign of the crew getting clear.
The tail gunner's sitting sideways, still strapped in.
That could be me. What sort of discipline

makes us too pig-headed to bale out?
I bet his instructions are the same as mine:
"It's no disgrace to quit a crippled plane.
Why do you think we give you parachutes?
Action's no different from an exercise."
That's what the Group-Captain always says.

Once in a while he gives us this long spiel
on all the public investment spent on us
—makes me feel like a bloody council house.
It's his job to say that, but we know how he feels.
He's got medals down to here. He's seen the lot.
He never chickened out when it got hot.

The tail's sliding under ... It's completely gone
... not even a shadow underneath the sea.
Give the map reference to SOC.
It might not be too deep. Two hundred metres down?
The subs will move in fast—ours and the Soviets
—like bloody piranha to see what they can get.

If ours arrive first, they'll put two divers in
with underwater cameras. They won't try
to salvage anything—except logs and codes maybe.
Then plant a charge, blow it to smithereens,
and bugger off back the way they came.
If the Russians get there first, they'll do the same.

It's so quiet with them gone. They're still alive,
watching the fish outside, conscious of each sound
from the airframe, taking forever to drown.
That slow—ugh, I can feel it—that slow dive.
Christ, he's a Bear H! Did they flick the switch
to arm the warheads when they ditched?

We're carrying live missiles. Isn't he?
They can't risk blowing him up. We'd be nuts
to assume that concrete ballast's all he's got.
What'll the Russians do? Or MOD?
They can't leave a bomb on the seabed to rot.
Yes they can. It's the only choice they've got.

Phantom Cockpit. 0720 hours.

American Pilot:

Can't head back home yet. We have to check
for survivors. So do it . . . It's a waste of time.
It bugs me, the thought of dyin' so far from home,
like Marsha's brother in Vietnam.
These Russians were real people, family men, the same
as you and me . . . Let's go. There's no sign of the wreck.

This is the bit I hate. The sudden guilt
when it's all over. "Guilt and relief go together
—This message come to you from Marsha's quack."
He gets ninety bucks an hour to hear her yak!
She and I couldn't talk to one another
without arguing. "Your husband is self-willed,"

he'd say. "Pay the receptionist on the way out."
I've seen better advice in a fortune cookie.
How come two people with so much to share
can't talk straight or believe the other cares?
You thought I was always chasing nookie.
That's what you thought. So, that's how it worked out.

It's not full daylight yet. There's still some stars.
We're near the mainland . . . See the gantries on the coast?
Those dark flecks on the radar dish?
The storm did that. That's kelp, caught in the mesh.
It can cause false signals, radar ghosts,
'Chinese Whispers' in the corridors of power.

23

The Kremlin's smart. They won't conceal the crash.
Tass will say, with regret, a scheduled flight
from Russia to Cuba crashed at sea.
Only fifteen passengers. Wasn't that lucky?
The Ministry of Defence sure won't contradict.
It'll only last for one day in the press.

And yet for decades, maybe centuries to come,
that Bear's gonna lie on the Atlantic bed.
The sea'll tear old Rumbleguts apart,
corrode his brainbox, pump salt through his heart
till it gets a straight answer from the dead
and blurts it out . . . Look, we're nearly home.

That's the Eden estuary . . . sometimes . . . Goddamn,
I scare myself. I can't feel anger any more.
It's been drilled out of me. Discipline, training
—from "doolie" cadet in Colorado Springs
to damn near ten thousand flying hours.
I'm thirty-six years old. That's how I am.

Lower the landing gear . . . The sky's still red and gold
. . . Sea's sparkling like coins thrown on a table.
. . . Early-morning horsemen on the beach under us
. . . Runway's like a big St Andrew's cross.
There's Leuchars Church, where Marsha wasn't able
to think of anything but the cold.

We're down. I need breakfast. We've been gone three hours.
. . . See that F5 with Russian markings parked back there?
It's used as the aggressor for our training exercises
—a touch of realism. Realism! It flies
real well. I've flown it. I've played the Bear.
The guys like bein' the Bear . . . Cut engines . . . Switch off power

MELVILLE BAY

HULTON PICTURE LIBRARY

In the year 1838 a young ship's surgeon
tells the story of a whaling expedition
from Dundee to north-west Greenland.

1. Trying Out

Grey smoke rose through the Greenland sky all day
like surfacing breaths from an enormous whale.
On deck the cauldrons hissed and spat
while in the hold the cooling butts
thickened and slapped. The stiff folds of our sails
glistened with grease. In the crook of Melville Bay

a hard September sun set in the hills.
It coloured the snow red. The tryworks boiled,
as round the flames men spiked the strips
of blubber, filled the cauldrons up,
laughed and skated with their hooks where oil
had greased the deck. Black carcasses of whales

bobbed alongside in chains, all specked with snow,
till each was hauled on to the cutting stage.
The air hissed with flensing knives and claws;
bones squeaked and snapped beneath the saws.
The starboard bulwarks acted like a cage
for slippery flesh that slid towards the bows.

I was no sailor. It was my first time
on a whaleship. Captain Chalmers took me on
as his ship's surgeon because I
was half way through my medical degree.
Chalmers nodded: "That's half more than the last one.
If you can set a bone, you'll do just fine."

Five months out from Dundee, the fishy stench
no longer troubled me. Great ropes of smoke
twisted upwards from the cauldrons' mouths.
Hard by starboard, ice floes drifted south
or caught on headlands like white flowers on stalks.
Folco, the carpenter, stood at his bench

straightening saws and sharpening worked-out blades.
The owner's son, Paul Graham, smoked his pipe,
perched high up on the spare boat skids.
The boatswain Carey's baccy quid
bulged through his hare-lipped grin, each time we wiped
away the sweat, at the Indian streaks we made.

As it grew dark, we saw the esquimaux
venturing closer to the fiery glare.
Our masts and shrouds and close-furled sails
stood black above the molten whales.
Sparks flew like shooting stars through the night air.
Our fires drowned out the crackle of the floes.

A crescent moon watched as we hacked and hurled.
Sometimes we glimpsed beside the cabin stairs
two tall, cloaked women in fur hoods.
"Women don't bring a ship no good,"
muttered Folco. The captain's wife went to her prayers
and left the darkness to the other girl.

2. Pack Ice

In the morning, when the tryworks fires were out,
the sky shone twice as blue and twice as cold.
The yellow sun gave off no heat.
Frost crazed the deck beneath our feet.
Wisps of fishy steam seeped from the hold
for Reuben the cat to ruffle and sniff out.

We had the best catch. The rest of our fleet
had sailed from Melville Bay three days before
with holds half-empty. Graham had made us wait
till we had finished trying-out.
While Captain Chalmers rushed about and swore,
his wife rehearsed her hymns and stayed discreet.

The lower main hold was stacked high with casks
of whale oil and meat packed in layers of salt,
beside great bundles of baleen
for umbrella ribs and corset bones.
And in the fore 'tween decks lay sealskin pelts
coddled round heavy spermaceti flasks.

Paul Graham took a ledger round the holds
—his father's son—to tally all our catch,
checking it with his tall, young wife.
Folco ground out a ragged knife.
"Wives is bad luck," he grunted to the watch.
"Aye, and not just at sea," the cold watch growled.

The night had bound more ice-floes in the bay.
They creaked and tapped against the naked stem,
no longer fendered by our whales.
All morning we prepared to sail.
Five of us climbed down to hack ice from the stern.
Above, the ship's name glinted: *Mercury*.

We used the on-shore wind as best we could
and nosed our way between the grumbling floes.
The passage narrowed, disappeared.
Sun and wind dropped. The sky was clear
with gimlet stars. We felt our outer clothes
stiffen with frost as if we were made of wood.

The crew climbed down on to the ice with ropes
to haul the *Mercury* toward the sea.
The more we tugged, the more we slipped
and dragged ice up against the ship
till all our axes could not cut her free.
The silent women watched us climb back up.

3. The Whaleboats

Three days slipped by. Cracks opened in the ice
and sealed again more tightly. Hummocks rose.
The captain glumly led the men in morning prayers.
His wife's voice swooped through the air,
bearing our hymns across the echoing floes.
Paul Graham grew restless. At first his advice

was to keep trying to move the *Mercury*.
The captain told him that it was no use,
that we would have to winter here:
"We've stores to last us a whole year."
"My father won't take that for an excuse,"
snapped Graham. "He wants the oil. Who's going to pay?"

We'd little chance of catching up our fleet,
but Graham was determined to send word back home:
"Or, if we find a ship near here,
we'll transfer our cargo to her.
We've food enough, but we're too low on rum.
What will the men do when it runs out?"

The crew played cards. I cut some whaletooth dice.
Folco taught young Isles to make scrimshaw.
Graham and the captain argued in full view
while Reuben prowled and Carey chewed.
The captain gave in: "Two whaleboats can go
and maybe find a ship beyond the ice."

Graham and the captain both agree to go.
Neither trusted the other out of sight.
Graham insisted he bring his wife with him,
so Mrs Chalmers came with her hymns.
Folco and Isles prepared to man Graham's boat.
The captain took Carey and the third mate, Low.

31

Each chose two seamen, long-boned Stromness lads
and watched while the whaleboats were loaded up
with casks of water, salt meat and oatmeal,
candles, rum, ice-saws, warm wraps made from seals.
Folco made decks and nailed canvas on top
then bolted sledge runners to the whaleboats' sides.

They went on board. The davits rattled out
and lowered them to the ice. The ladies sat
while the men hauled the boats along.
They stopped, looked up at us. Something was wrong.
The captain walked back, hailed John Cramb the mate:
"The ship's listing. I can see it from the boat."

Our deck seemed flat enough. I placed a penny
on its edge. The crew watched it slowly roll
to the port side and clatter down.
"I'm sending Folco back again"
the captain called. "He'll need to brace the hull.
I'll take you instead." He pointed at me.

4. The Journey South

I ran below and filled my ditty bag
with medical supplies. The rest I gave to Cramb.
I took Folco's rope. We made our way
south by south west on Melville Bay.
Although the ice was ridged where floes had jammed,
we'd no deep snow to make our runners drag.

Despite the cold, I soon worked up a sweat
and felt it stick and freeze on my eyebrows.
Crystals of ice, like frozen tears,
clung to my lashes and my beard.
The whaleboats handled like two clumsy scows.
We raised the masts but no wind filled our sheets.

The ice grew rougher. Jagged, rockswept slopes
forced us east to find a passable route.
One smooth field slithered down into a ditch.
Another petered out in treacherous brash.
Twice we had to carry the whaleboats
between locked bergs that frayed our frozen ropes.

When sun and moon stood in the same sky
we pitched camp in our boats. Mrs Chalmers asked:
"Whom would you like mentioned in your prayers?"
"I pray we meet no polar bears,"
grinned Carey. All night long the salt meat casks
creaked if we stirred, so close-packed did we lie.

Beside me lay an oilskin lucifer bag
and a box of maroons. The saltpetre smell
made me dream of Coronation Day
and the fireworks I saw as a boy.
Our sealskin wraps were cold as chestnut shells.
Mrs Graham's pillow was a folded flag.

The morning saw us stiff as marionettes.
Captain Chalmers was all for turning round:
"There's no point struggling on," he said. "We're not equipped."
"We've come this far. Let's try to find a ship,"
Graham argued."Look! I can see an open sound."
We hacked the runners free and off we set.

The ice grew smooth. A wind rose. The boats skimmed
and bumped across the ice with bulging sails.
We reached a channel, launched the boats.
Our legs felt strange to be afloat.
We saw no ships. An anvil-headed gale
struck towards us. The sky grew tallow dim.

The wind dropped suddenly. We tried to row
back to the shore. We heard a humming noise
that become a whistle. The sky had grown
a luminous blue-black. The air pressed down.
Waves pushed the boats apart. I heard my voice
shout to Mrs Graham to keep down low.

5. The Storm

We dropped our sails and hugged the ragged shore,
but the storm clutched and tore us out to sea.
Our whaleboats seemed to shrink. The waves
became a seething labyrinth of caves.
I was hurled to the gunwales. Above me,
the Stromness men fought with the steering oar.

It sprang loose and was gone. The whaleboat yawed.
Disaster, when it came, came suddenly.
The captain's boat leaped at a floe
that sheared the mast, stove in her prow
and sucked her under. Paul Graham braced his knee
like a harpooner. He crashed overboard.

Our Stromness men drowned, trying to save him.
I tried to bale. A barrel crushed Isles' chest.
My lint was soaked and would not staunch his blood.
Breached stores clung to my boots like mud.
The whaleboat teetered on a great wave's crest
where screeching sleet tore at my eyelids' skin.

The whole weight of the the wave dropped on the boat.
I grasped the steering-oar brace. Mrs Graham
clung to my waist. Isles' body flew,
like a doll with its head askew,
up through the water. The boat's frame
shuddered and righted. We began to float,

mastless and oarless on the rolling caps
as the storm died away. Mrs Graham and I
baled out the hull. Our stores were soaked.
Worst of all, our water casks were breached
and mingled with brine. Our own clothes seemed dry,
till we stopped working. We piled up the wraps

and huddled together. We could not speak.
I tried to keep myself from falling asleep
I salvaged some oatmeal. It smelled of brine.
I made her eat it. The sun began to shine.
It gave no heat. I looked out for a ship,
but all that moved were icebergs' glittering peaks.

She gathered strength and talked. She had been wed
less than a year. Their families were close friends.
She had known him all her life,
always assumed she'd be his wife.
She'd seen him sail away, come back again
"looking more like himself each trip he made,

less like his father," she said. "He'd always try
to teach me. This voyage to Greenland
was his idea. He wanted me to see
and not be like those women at the quay,
afraid of what they do not understand."
I realised she was as young as I.

Five days we drifted, waterless. We ate
as little as we could of the salt food.
She became delirious. All I could do
was bleed her. I gathered her blood in a shoe,
mixed it with meal and fed her. The fresh blood
revived her. I bled myself and ate.

I dried the lucifers inside my shirt
and shook out powder from the wet maroons.
At dusk we saw a sail. I lit a fire,
fed it with damp pelts. The smoke rose higher
till we were seen. It was a Dutch ship, the Jan Boom.
They launched a boat and carried us on board.

6. Laura Graham

The Dutchman gave us warm, dry clothes.
His Malay cook made us a court bouillon,
laced with genever. We inhaled its heat
and told our story. He agreed
to take us to the port of Godhavn,
but wouldn't risk his ship in more rescues.

Two days of keen wind let us make good speed.
We rounded the bleak cliffs of Svarten Huk
and spied three whaleships nestling by the cape.
I took the captain's telescope,
read their names and called Mrs Graham to look:
Sidlaw, Chattan, Pointer—our own fleet.

I went aboard the *Chattan*. Even as I climbed
up the rope ladder, watched by the whole crew,
word spread that the *Mercury* was lost.
I told them, "No." Old James Buist,
the senior captain, called the other two.
He said, if we sailed now, there should be time

to take survivors off the *Mercury*
before fresh sea-ice blocked the shore again.
We sailed. The storm had scoured the coast,
changing its outline. Bergs and floes
slipped by. Buist insisted Mrs Graham
should take his cabin. For six nights she lay

burning with fever. She would talk and doze,
call Paul Graham's name, ask me not to leave her.
The *Chattan's* surgeon, Donald Grier,
looked at her once, would not go near,
mumbling, "It could be scarlet fever,"
despite the violet frostbite on her toes.

By the time the fleet made Melville Bay
the worst of Laura Graham's illness was past.
She'd hardly strength to stir her sheets,
but joked about her bandaged feet,
"I shall not dance again with Mr Frost."
I only smiled, unsure of what to say.

The five days' icy drift seemed far away.
Laura had the warmth of a real bed,
water to drink and the captain's best food.
Our sealskin huddle and the taste of blood
seemed like some indiscretion, best unsaid.
I rose to leave. She motioned to me to stay.

She seemed to take on her widow's role
as if she and Paul Graham had talked it through.
"My voyage," she said, "is already done."
She raised her head, "But yours is just begun."
I'd been too close to say it wasn't true.
We were like twins, too bonded to console.

Her hands were cold. I laid her hooded cloak
over the bed, like the doctor I would be.
She drifted off to sleep again.
I heard the sound of anchor chains
and footsteps on the stairs. I went to see.
The captain's steward called me to the boats.

7. The Mercury

The three whaleships dropped anchor well off shore.
We took eight whaleboats, each manned with four men
to leave space for the stranded crew.
By the map we'd just four miles to go
across the ice. The black whaleboats began
to crawl like beetles on a dairy floor.

The sun set early. Through a cold, red mist
we heard a dull boom, then quick rifle fire.
As the haze sank, the *Mercury*
loomed like a wave of crystal spray.
These were no shots, but the crack of timber.
The pack had crushed her sides. The penny list

had heeled so far her yardarms scraped the floe.
The tryworks stared like blind eyes from the deck.
Davits curled down like walrus teeth
with tight-lipped chain plate mouths beneath.
As we drew close we made out, round the wreck,
oil-barrels stacked but no sign of the crew.

We hailed the *Mercury*. No answer came.
The hatches gaped like grizzled men struck dumb.
Then slowly from the barrel stacks
figures appeared; voices called back.
Folco was waving, and the mate John Cramb.
More cracks rang out round the port anchor chain.

Folco had built the barrels into huts,
lined with sail canvas. When we went inside
we found men huddled round a stove.
Folco embraced me with his tattered gloves.
Somehow they knew Captain Chalmers had died
before I told them. From the low roof struts

hung a lantern, unlit to save oil
amid the plenty. We bundled up in sealskin pelts,
afraid to fall too much asleep.
We rose before the sun came up.
Cramb gave the order to strike camp. I knelt
and helped lash up the sealskins into bales.

We loaded all we could into the boats:
whaletooth, seal pelts, spermaceti flasks.
Folco had made skids for the baleen
and rigged them up with a lateen.
We left behind most of the whale oil casks.
As we looked back, we saw the frail huts float,

like makeshift coracles, above the mist.
The Mercury's hull seemed a hummocked floe.
Folco, now that his work was done,
looked like an old man, small, withdrawn.
We reached the *Chattan* in a swirling snow.
Cramb and I made reports to Captain Buist.

I went to Laura. She sat up in bed
and asked me, one by one, about the crew.
She listened gravely, as her husband's heir,
inquired about the cargo, "I declare,
when I go home, I'll have much work to do."
She lay back down. I smoothed the patchwork spread.

I sat with Laura till she fell asleep
then went on deck and watched the moonlit clouds
massing. While the fleet prepared to sail
from Melville Bay, a school of whales
played under the full moon off the starboard bow,
silently sounding out our southbound ships.

THE OTHER THIEF

A burglar has one particular house
as his target. He has brought a
new accomplice.

1.
Keep your voice down until we get inside.
A street like this has far more than its share
of nosy neighbours, women who can't sleep
and business types with bad accounts to keep.
Wait here. Sounds carry further in night air
and moonlight makes your movements magnified.

You stay by the garage. Their car's not there
—always check that. I'll try out the back door.
Keep a look-out. D'you mind me telling you
—it's just a habit—saying what to do.
I know you haven't tried this game before.
One: don't get greedy. Two: stay aware

—that's all you need to earn yourself the breaks.
Right, here I go. There's no alarm box
that I can see. But still I'll double check
for contact-breakers. Never risk your neck.
There may be cameras triggered by the locks.
or infra-red beams. Wait. I'll be right back.

What have we got? No systems anyhow.
The back door's solid and it has a Chubb.
The kitchen window has a shaky catch.
The side-porch door's half off the latch;
the frame has woodworm round about the snib.
That's the way in. Wait. That's it. Let's go.

2.
Close the door tight behind you. Check it's shut.
Doors can creak and bang on windless nights.
Watch your feet beside that box of logs.
See that dog basket? You can tell their dog
has gone with them by how that blanket sits.
What's this? Another basket? No, a cot

with a dolly out of favour with her mum
—didn't get to go on holiday
with the family. Hello there. What's your name?
All right. Don't be so jumpy. We've got time.
I told you I know this house. OK? OK?
I told you I used to live here, chum.

Don't worry. I'm not here for sentiment.
I'm here for money. These people are rich
—good luck to them. And good luck, what's-your-name.
May your insurance satisfy your claim.
Pass me some wire. Let's see which lock is which
on that inner door. They're old. They'd not prevent

a dog from walking in. They're hardly caught.
The cylinders are loose, the springs are weak.
I don't even need wire. I'll use a card.
There. That's one open. The other's a bit hard.
I'll use the wire. Shhh! What was that click?
It's just the porch door. Try to wedge it shut.

You know how, when you're small, everything looks big?
Well, now this house feels really small to me.
It's funny though. It starts songs in my head.
All right. I'll think about the lock instead.
There it goes. Just like I had my own key.
Home again, home again, jiggity-jig.

3.
Let's try the kitchen, That's good. The moon throws
more light in here. Don't use torches. We've enough
to see. I'll check the cupboards. You do drawers.
And only take just what we're looking for:
cash, credit cards, jewels—no bulky stuff.
Don't slow yourself down with that radio.

One thing about the self-employed that's nice:
half of them don't report it when they're robbed
—not if you just take cash. They'd have to face
questions on why it's here in the first place.
All of us self-employed do similar jobs.
Only wage-earners like to be precise.

All right. I'll keep my voice down. Yes. All right.
My father always said I was too loud.
My mother didn't mind, though. I spent hours
in here while she baked or arranged flowers.
She'd only shout when Dad's boots brought in mud
from the garden. She kept this floor so bright

you could see the underside of Dinky cars.
They've got good glass and fancy casseroles
—no good to me unless I still lived here.
What's that you've found? They're just four-packs of beer.
Leave them. Take bottles of spirits—if they're full.
Was there nothing worth having in the drawers?

Women sometimes keep spare cash around
in the fridge. No burglar would look there,
they think. Why should a housewife know
any more than she's told on radio?
Of course I'm fair to women. Thank you dear.
See—here in the crisper—thirty pounds.

4.
The back hall smells the same: flues from the stove,
stale polish, coir doormat and cold glass.
I thought it would have changed. They've kept that row
of maids' bells. We'd no maids. All right. I know
it's just a house. These door handles are brass
—worst thing for fingerprints. Keep on your gloves.

Don't waste time there. That's just a scullery.
It's not? What is it, then? A bathroom? Well,
so it should be. We should have done that.
I remember, once in summer, a young bat
flew in among the jars and pans. It crawled
and flapped for hours till my Dad set it free.

The pantry's still a pantry. They have wine
where we'd an apple barrel. That freezer chest
is worth a look. I once found one transformed
into a wage safe—that was on a farm.
'Course I've done farms. You're stupid if you rest
in town. Take that suitcase to put things in.

The freezer's full of food? Too bad. Come on.
Wait. What's that long box up there on the wall?
It's padlocked. Can you reach it from the chair?
No, best forget it. I know what's in there.
That's a gun case. I don't touch them at all.
The cops don't give up when it comes to guns.

Don't look at me like that. This is routine.
It's burglary. They just file a report.
But if the cops think that a gun's involved,
the pressure's turned on them to get it solved.
You haven't brought one, have you? If we're caught
. . . don't ever do that again. Know what I mean?

5.
Look how the woodwork changes in the hall:
plain pine for servants, oak for the middle-class.
See, the barometer's going up—
set fair for us. Hey, easy, mind your step.
Let's see if they've set pressure pads for us.
No. The carpet's smooth. They've none at all.

I should have told you—though it's quite rare still—
sometimes you get a house with infra-red.
Detectors cost a lot, though, so they're placed
where their fish-eye can cover a wide space.
I can show you how to fool them. What you need
is education. Think of this as night-school.

Remember, we may need time to escape.
Go to the front door and lock the catch
on the Yale. That way no-one can get inside.
You saw me do it at the back and side.
You didn't? You won't learn unless you watch.
Have I been caught? Never. Touch wood. Don't tempt fate.

That's a nice mirror. Wait. What did you say?
What makes you think I've ever been in jail?
I thought you were new here. Anyway, it's true.
Not jail, exactly. Nothing to do
with this sort of game. It's bad for the morale,
this prison talk. Let's get on with it, eh?

Don't go upstairs yet. He'll have a desk. We'll look
down here first. Why is it gates and doors
make you stop and shuffle through your thoughts?
They don't do that to you? Well, maybe not.
This hall once had a wooden parquet floor.
I could hear every step my father made.

6.
This is the dining-room. The moon's so bright
you could eat by it. Take those candlesticks.
They're old. We're in luck. Look at the hallmark.
They're solid. That fire used to spit and spark
—rude noises at dinner. All right. I'll be quick.
It's not an in-and-out. We've time at night

when the house is empty. Don't make a mess.
If we're tidy, it could take them days
to realise that someone's been in here.
They'll think things are mislaid, not disappeared.
They don't know their own homes. You'd be amazed
how few remember half what they possess.

At first my parents entertained a lot.
When I was little I had party food
for lunch and dinner on the following days.
Take that carriage clock. Treat it carefully.
Wrap it up in a tablecloth. That's good.
Shhh! That's a car. It's stopping ... No, it's not.

We'll take these spoons. Take that salt cellar too.
It may not look much. It's worth eighty quid.
Trust me. Relax. You're doing really well.
You're learning. It takes experience to tell
what's worth having. We're not just young kids
who take out TV sets and videos

and get ripped off themselves by bigger crooks.
My father loved these parties. He had style,
real charm. He found it easy to persuade.
Despite yourself, you'd agree with what he said.
He'd a temper, though, beneath that smile.
He once cracked this door panel—look.

7.
Here's the study. Why isn't there a desk?
The filing cabinet's not even locked.
I'll check the drawers to see if I can find
anything negotiable. Never mind
what that means. You look through the shelves of books
for dummies. No, that one's just a flask.

You're quick, though. You'll do well. Got what it takes.
to size things up. A few more times like this
and you'll be telling me what to do.
No, I didn't start as young as you.
Wait. Give all that computer stuff a miss.
No-one will buy it. You should only take

things you can get rid of the same day.
Never be stuck with keeping stuff at home.
When dealers know you, you'll get a fair price
if you're a regular. Think about my advice
—you won't get rich, but you'll have a safe income.
The greedy ones get caught and put away.

Here's something just for you. The perfect book:
'A Guide to Antique Silver'. Stick it in.
I'm not kidding. Or would you like to own
'Housebreaking for Beginners'? Hey, calm down.
Where's your humour? Take that violin.
I remember how my father used to look

when she played the piano just for him.
What? Not my mother. Someone else.
Here, try to open this box. What's that knife?
You took it from the kitchen. I believe
you're too fond of weapons. What the hell's . . .
it's just that wrapped-up clock trying to chime.

8.
Let's try the drawing-room. What have they done?
It's nearly empty. Everything is white:
white carpets, curtains. They even have white chairs.
I bet they don't allow a child in here.
It's like a magazine. On winter's nights
we used to sit in here with the shutters drawn.

We had a long couch here. Dad's armchair
was by the right side of—a different fire.
My mother's chair ... Yes, I'm all right. I'm fine.
What's that huge plant? Some kind of creeping vine.
How can they live in here? I'd soon get tired
of all this nothing. There's some silver? Where?

That vase is good. Let's see it. No. Too bad.
So that's what his gun's for—clay pigeon shoots.
You can't take trophies. They're too easily traced.
We won't find anything in this place.
What? You like this room best? Goes with your suit?
Very funny. I wish they'd half the things we had.

If we were rich, why am I a thief
—you want to know? Maybe some other time.
It's a mixture of bad luck and mistakes.
Well, what else would it be? It doesn't take
much to go broke. Social history of crime,
is it? Classic study: good family come to grief.

How much do you know? Who've you talked to?
Well, if you knew the truth, you'd not be here.
No, never mind. I meant nothing by that.
Come on. We're wasting time with too much chat.
I said I'd train you for your new career.
Doing my bit for the unemployed, you know.

9.
Look how the moonlight slants across the stairs.
This staircase used to seem so high and wide.
I had dreams about it. I must have been
four or five years old. Something slow and green
—crocodile-snake—would come. I'd hear it slide
and race it to my parents' bed, dead scared.

I suppose most kids have dreams like that.
You didn't? Well, you wouldn't. You got missed
when imagination was dealt out.
Calm down. Let go my arm, and watch your mouth.
Don't be so jumpy. Let go of my wrist.
If you act like this someone will knock you flat.

Lucky I don't get roused. If I were you
I'd learn to keep the head. If you can't stand
the pressure, you won't last long in this game.
OK, maybe I am a bit to blame.
I talk too much. This patter—understand?—
keeps me relaxed. Don't let it get to you.

See where the stair turns. We'd a mirror there.
My father would sort his tie or check his shoes.
He'd look at himself and never smile at all
—saved that for others. You could see the hall
from the landing, but no-one could see you
because of the shadow from the chandelier.

That's how I saw them, how I first found out.
I don't know how I'd been naive so long.
What did you say? You're right. We've got to move.
It was the way that he said 'love'.
OK. I'm coming. No, there's nothing wrong.
Nothing you need to worry about.

10
This is my parents' bedroom. That's their bed.
It feels so empty when he stays out late.
My mother always waits up till he comes home.
She can't sit still. She'll work until he comes.
She dusts the mantlepiece while she waits,
polishes mirrors, rubs gilt frames till they're red.

Shhh. She'll hear us. Hey, let go my arm.
What do you mean, this talk gives you the creeps?
Sorry. I just felt it. I'll be all right soon.
I'm being silly. Blame it on the moon.
You're cold. Let's finish. We should be asleep.
What's that in your coat? You'll come to less harm

without a gun. A gun may make you brave.
You only mean to use it as a threat.
But what do you do when someone calls your bluff
and walks towards you? Do you . . . That's enough.
We haven't even looked for jewels yet.
Look at me shaking. That's no way to behave.

Forget what I said about being neat.
We've taken things that they'll miss right away.
Empty the chest of drawers. Look for a box.
Look, here's a good watch tucked in with his socks.
What's that you've got? Ah, we're in luck today.
Beginner's luck. Don't bet on a repeat.

Look at this sapphire ring. It's not a fake.
You only see that setting if it's real.
That clasp . . . those pearls . . . take the whole box along.
The lady has good taste. Don't get me wrong:
it's not that guns frighten me at all,
just that I've seen the mess that they can make.

11.
Don't bother with the bathroom. Oh, I forgot.
you like your pills. Go on. Keep on your gloves.
I wouldn't know what I was looking for.
What are you do . . . ? Who's that behind the door?
It's just a dressing gown. The way it moved,
I thought . . . So did you. It nearly got shot.

51

Let me have the gun. You nearly blew it then.
One shot and you'd wake up the whole street.
I'll give it back when we get out of here.
OK? I won't keep it. No bloody fear.
It's worse for me if I get caught with it.
That's right. Like you say, something with a gun

—that's why I was inside. I was just a kid.
Yes, much younger than you. Only fifteen.
It was a shotgun, not a thing like this.
Look, it's safe in my pocket. What's that hiss?
Stop playing with that perfume spray, you queen.
Hey, don't be so jumpy. Keep the head.

I hope whatever these pills are calm you down.
You're something else. I thought that *I* was tense.
Tell you the rest? Well, I just lost my head.
I was a kid. Yes, someone wound up dead.
No, the lawyer couldn't call it self-defence.
We had a bath so big a horse could drown

—a big Victorian bath on iron feet
not like that puny little plastic tub.
What's wrong? You want me to tell you the rest?
You make me feel I'm stealing my own past
in this house. No, I did not kill in cold blood.
He was cold blooded. I was the opposite.

12.
Come in here. It's dark. Where is the moon?
It used to shine in here. I know it did.
I wasn't dreaming. I was wide awake.
Shut up. Shut up. For once give me a break.
I should know where it was I lay and hid.
Not then. I was a kid. This is my room.

My room. My door. My window. And my bed.
You haven't listened. Don't know what it's about,
what prison does to how you feel a place.
Shut up. Get that torch out of my face.
You need it spelled out? I'll spell it out.
I've said who I killed. I've told you who's dead.

You make it hard for me, hard for yourself.
Do you think I like to say it now?
I came home early. I came home.
Got that? Picture that? Me in school uniform.
I came up to this room. I didn't know.
Shut up and let me finish it myself.

They were in the north bedroom. I could hear.
The door was half ajar. All I could see
was their clothes on the floor. I ran downstairs
into the kitchen. There was a dead hare
on the table. His gun and keys,
a box of cartridges. The dead hare's ear

was oozing blood. Shut up. You started me.
You wanted it. You're going to hear it all.
I loaded the gun and pushed open the door.
I'd never seen a woman naked before.
She saw me first and cowered against the wall.
My father knelt back and looked at me.

13.
He looked at me the way he used to look
at his own face in the mirror on the stair.
No expression, just a look to see
what was needed. He said nothing to me
—just got up and walked across, not scared.
I said 'Stop?', He kept coming. My hand shook.

Shut up. Come back here. Don't go into that room.
That's where it happened. My hand shook, I said.
Don't you believe that a child's hand can shake?
It happened so quickly. He fell back
on to the bed beside her. The sheets turned red.
I see you. Stand up. Look at that moon.

It's making fun of us. When you were small,
did you believe in the Man in the Moon?. I did.
No, kids like you never had a chance.
It was explored already. No romance.
Well, I believed in romance as a kid
—Biggles and Santa Claus and Sunday School.

I was a good boy. I did as I was told.
No, wait. I haven't finished. You get back.
Look what you've done. You've dropped the bloody case.
The clock is smashed. Spoons all over the place.
What? D'you think you're going to be attacked?
D'you think I'm mad? No, I'm just growing old.

Let's go. That noise was good as an alarm.
It was my mother's face I can't forget
—down the staircase—the last thing that I saw
—out the way we came—was her at the window,
comforting, wiping away the tears and sweat,
holding the other woman in her arms.

RADIO POEMS

All these poems were written for the spoken voice, allowing for music and sound effects. I try to use verse forms with a strong structure of rhyme and rhythms which keeps the narrative moving, but is flexible enough to let actors vary the pace and mood, deliver punch lines etc. The language is intended to allow scope for actors to bring their own characterisation to the pieces. I did some rewriting in studio during recordings, just as one would with a film script.

These three documentary poems are based on fact, but certain details have been altered to protect individual privacy.

CHASING THE BEAR

I am grateful to the US Air Force Academy in Colorado Springs and RAF Leuchars for allowing me to visit and providing invaluable information. US Freedom of Information legislation allows much material regarding NATO defences to be publicly accessible in the USA. The UK is much more restrictive as are the Warsaw Pact countries. BBC Scotland has suffered police raids following the making of programmes on topics affecting national security. So far, alone among my radio poems, *Chasing the Bear* has not been considered acceptable for broadcast.

MELVILLE BAY

When I first saw Greenland from the air in 1965, its icy coastline made me want to write about it. My mother's family comes from Dundee where there is a legacy of whaling stories. For personal reasons, my interest was not in the hunt but in the deep bonding that can occur between those who survive a tragedy. *Melville Bay* was produced for BBC Radio by John Arnott who commissioned an original musical score from the composer Malcolm Clarke. The narrator was Alan Cumming.

THE OTHER THIEF

I grew up in a house like the one in the poem. I taught for some years at John Jay College of Criminal Justice in New York. I learned rather more in Hackney. My concern in this story is for the extreme violence of the innocent. *The Other Thief* was produced for BBC Radio by John Arnott, using binaural sound to create the illusion that the listener is drawn through the house as the thief's accomplice. The actor was Bill Paterson.

— **Robin Bell**